T0208351

The Great End Time Deception Exposed

DANIEL HEYNIKE

WESTBOW
PRESS®
A DIVISION OF THOMAS NELSON
& ZONDERVAN

WestBow Press books may be ordered through booksellers or by contacting:

WestBow Press
A Division of Thomas Nelson & Zondervan
1663 Liberty Drive
Bloomington, IN 47403
www.westbowpress.com
1 (866) 928-1240

Scripture taken from the King James Version of the Bible.

ISBN: 978-1-9736-7037-7 (sc)
ISBN: 978-1-9736-7036-0 (e)

Print information available on the last page.

WestBow Press rev. date: 9/11/2019

CONTENTS

1

CHAPTER

THE GREAT END TIME DECEPTION EXPOSED

INTRODUCTION

The great deception foretold by Jesus in Mathew 24v24 will be like the one which led to his crucifixion when the Jews misread Jesus's intentions and placed their hope in him raising an army and defeating the Romans. In their disappointment they turned on him and helped the priests to crucify him.

Ninety five percent or more of the world's greatest Bible believing teachers and evangelists today teach (I know only one that does not) that born-again Christians have nothing to fear as they will be raptured prior to the great tribulation and thus escape it. Imagine the disappointment, disillusionment and fear that will arise when all these unprepared Christians learn that these great leaders have deceived them, and they will have to wait till the very last hour of the very last day and possibly even the very last minute of the end of the age before they are saved by joining their Lord in the sky. Instead of escaping without a scratch the deceived and unprepared Christians will have to endure the worst time of tribulation to date. Jesus warns us of this time in Mat 24v8 & 9 when many Christians will "be offended, and shall betray one another, and shall hate one another" when they suddenly find that Christians are hated by all nations and they are going to be afflicted and even killed if they confess to being followers of Jesus. Hence Jesus's warning in Mat 24v10 that many will be offended by end time events, grow cold and lose their salvation.

Since Jesus cannot lie, this deception will take place, and many will be lost. Jesus also said in Mat 24v13 that "he that shall endure unto the end, the same shall be saved". It is therefore my earnest desire and prayer that the truth be revealed prior to the event so many may escape this end time deception by being prepared for it.

Over the last 41 years of my Christian walk I have developed a burden for those who will be lost in this end time deception and have studied earnestly to understand the reasons for this event and this is what I have learnt.

THE GREAT END TIME DECEPTION UNVEILED.

SETTING AND TIME

First the setting and time of this deception needs to be clearly understood. In Mathew 24v4 Jesus is answering the disciples when they asked, "Tell us, when shall these things be? and what shall be the sign of thy coming, and of the end of the world?". Here my KJV Bible says that "end of the world?" can also be read "end of the age". Jesus in his answer does not mention the words 'age' or 'world' but just "the end" but we know from Rev 21:1 "I saw a new heaven and a new earth: for the first heaven and the first earth were passed away" that the end of the world only occurs just before the new Jerusalem descends from heaven. Hence, they are all talking about the END OF THE AGE and not the end of the world. Here the END OF THE AGE also needs to be clearly understood. It is like the end of a dynasty or empire when the rulership of an area moves to another place or nation or new rulers. GOD has intervened many times in the affairs of men and nations. To mention just a few, there was the flood, the fall of Babylon and the Exodus from Egypt, but although these were great and serious events,

God did not revoke the authority he gave to Adam and his seed to reign and rule over the earth. When Adam and Eve took Satan's advice, they lost the Garden of Eden and pain, sin, toil and confusion became the lot of man. Man's conduct with the help of Satan eventually destroys the earth (Rev 11v18) and finally allows Satan to take complete control of it. The END OF THE AGE occurs when GOD calls an end to Man and Satan's joint reign, retakes control of the earth, and then pours out his judgment on it. This is not a period of days or weeks but a single moment in time.

THE SO CALLED GREAT TRIBULATION

Then we now need to understand and define the GREAT TRIBULATION. Most bible commentators define the GREAT tribulation as a 7 year period prior to Jesus's return to earth at Jerusalem starting with a 7 year peace covenant. This is not a very accurate description of this time and it needs to be looked at much more closely. Firstly, TRIBULATION means trouble or suffering and does not include an indication of where it comes from. Tribulation is mentioned 22 times in the KJV, 3 times in the old testament and 19 times in the new. Great Tribulation is only mentioned 4 times, once as much tribulation and 3 times as great tribulation. In Rev 2:18-22 God says to Jezebel at Thyatira that He will "cast her" and "them that commit adultery with her into great tribulation". Acts 14:22 says "that we must through much tribulation enter into the kingdom of God". In Rev 7:13-14 the elder points out the redeemed "which came out of great tribulation". The greatest tribulation that will ever be is only mentioned once in scripture: Matt 24:21 "For then shall be great tribulation, such as was not since the beginning of the world to this time, no, nor ever shall be." I will deal with this in depth below.

Persecution and tribulation are the lot of every servant of God. Job suffered great tribulation, John the Baptist had his head removed, Jesus was more marred than any man in addition to suffering the cross, Paul was stoned and left for dead more than once etc. Great Tribulation is still happening every day. The Centre for the Study of Global Christianity estimates that between the years 2005 and 2015, 900,000 Christians were martyred — an average of 90,000 Christians each year. There have always been "great" tribulations, from Adam and Eve being thrown out of the Garden of Eden and having to sow among the thorns, till now. All the above could testify to suffering GREAT TRIBULATION. It is therefore not easy to distinguish between tribulation and great tribulation. What we can say is that all the above (except for the flood) were regional tribulations and the only great change has been the population growth of both Christians and Gentiles leading to a massive increase in the number of the annual incidences mentioned above.

The bible warns, however, that a new time of GREAT GLOBAL TRIBULATIONS is coming. We read in Rev 6:8 "And power was given unto them over the fourth part of the earth, to kill with sword, and with hunger, and with death, and with the beasts of the earth". Also, in Rev 8:9 "And the third part of the creatures which were in the sea, and had life, died; and the third part of the ships were destroyed". These are all GREAT GLOBAL TRIBULATIONS and we are forewarned these are coming by Jesus in Matt 24:15: when he says "When ye therefore shall see the abomination of desolation, spoken of by Daniel the prophet, stand in the holy place, and Matt 24:21 "For then shall be great tribulation, such as was not since the beginning of the world to this time, no, nor ever shall be." From the above we can categorise GREAT TRIBULATION into three categories, GREAT REGIONAL TRIBULATION happening before the end times, GREAT GLOBAL TRIBULATION, world wars etc also happening before the end times and THE GREATEST GLOBAL TRIBULATION EVER, happening during the end times.

SEPARATING THE GREAT GLOBAL TRIBULATION FROM THE GREATEST GLOBAL TRIBULATION EVER

We are now able to separate the times of GLOBAL TRIBULATION into two identifiable periods, GREAT

GLOBAL TRIBULATION and the GREATEST GLOBAL TRIBULATION EVER.

Dealing with the greatest global tribulation ever first. In Matt 24:21 Jesus tells of the **greatest** tribulation that will ever be. Matt 24:15: says "When ye therefore shall see the abomination of desolation, spoken of by Daniel the prophet, stand in the holy place, and Matt 24:21 "For then shall be great tribulation, such as was not since the beginning of the world to this time, no, nor ever shall be." Daniel speaks of this time in Dan 9:27 "And he shall confirm the covenant with many for one week: and in the midst of the week he shall cause the sacrifice and the oblation to cease, and for the overspreading of abominations he shall make it desolate, even until the consummation, and that determined shall be poured upon the desolate." From this we understand that the Antichrist will establish a 7 year covenant with Israel and break it in the middle of the 7 year period when he causes the daily sacrifice and oblation to cease in Jerusalem.

Daniel also confirms the period of 3.5 years in Daniel 12v11: "from the time that the daily sacrifice is taken away, and the abomination of desolation is set up, there shall be one thousand two hundred and ninety days" (or 43 months, or 3 and a half years). We can determine from the beginning of Daniel Chapter 12 that this is the length of the period commonly referred to as Jacobs trouble. Verse 1 tells us that the Archangel Gabriel "the great prince who stands watch over the sons of your people" stands up "and there shall be a time of trouble, such as never was since there was a nation, Even to that time". So, we can now say that we have defined the period of GREATEST GLOBAL TRIBULATION EVER, it is the 3.5 year period after the Jews see the abomination of desolation in the Temple at Jerusalem. GREAT GLOBAL TRIBULATION occurs in the period prior to this.

We can now confirm that a 7 year period of great tribulation at or before the end times does not exist and originates out of a twisting or misunderstanding of the scriptures. This is bad news for all those born-again believers who have been led to believe the lie that they will not have to face THE GREAT TRIBULATION because they will be raptured away before that happens.

DISCUSSION

To understand how the great deception outlined above could have arisen we just have to look at Peter's failure to comprehend and agree to it being done Jesus' way. Peter was overjoyed that God in the form of Jesus had come in the flesh to forgive his sin, heal the sick and save Israel from its Roman overlords. He could not believe that when Jesus said he must die and rise again, that God could be killed. Hence, he rejected God's way for his way, which was to prevent Jesus being taken and killed. So he took a sword and detached the High Priest's servant's right ear in his attempt to prevent Jesus being taken. (John 18:10 Then Simon Peter having a sword drew it, and smote the high priest's servant, and cut off his right ear.) Here we see Peter getting it totally wrong by putting his will first. Although his assumption was correct that God could not be killed, (John 19:11 "Jesus answered, Thou couldest have no power at all against me, except it were given thee from above") it was putting his will first and refusing to accept the Lord's will that caused his offence so that Jesus turned, and said unto Peter "Get thee behind me, Satan: thou art an offence unto me: for thou savourest not the things that be of God, but those that be of men" Matt 16:23.

In the same way Peter was deceived, Satan uses our desire to please our congregations and to keep them coming and the income they bring. by presupposing the will of God without checking it with the Holy Spirit.

Having disclosed the great deception, born again believers who have been deceived, now have to reorganize their beliefs and their trust in the Lord. The best and only way to do this is to know the truth about the end time events. It requires a lot of dedicated study and help from the Holy Spirt to discern the truth about this time. But don't despair because Jesus wants you to know and left us a wealth of information, even to the extent that when we are closer to the event, we may be able to know the month of and even the exact day the Rapture. More of this later.

This leads us into the next chapter where we disclose the end time events and their timing as well as the Lord's instructions to help all born-again believers who will have to face the real possibility of great tribulation before they will be raptured away.

2
CHAPTER

THE EVENTS AND TIMING OF THE RAPTURE

PREAMBLE

In order for most of the born-again believers to be able to follow the narrative which follows, some of the rules of how the book the "Revelation of Jesus Christ" has been viewed for interpretation purposes follow:

From Rev 1:v10 & 11 "I was in the Spirit on the Lord's day, and heard behind me a great voice, as of a trumpet......Saying, I am Alpha and Omega, the first and the last: and, What thou seest, write in a book, and send it unto the seven churches...." we understand that while John was in the spirit praying he heard a voice behind him giving him instructions to write down what he saw. In this case Jesus was speaking. In other cases, an angel: Rev 5:2 "And I saw a strong angel proclaiming with a loud voice, Who is worthy to open the book…"

Rule 1: Text.
The text is the easiest to interpret. It says what it says but we must establish in each case who said it.

Rev 18: v1 "And **after** these things I saw another angel come down from heaven,…"

The book of Revelation is mostly in time order or sequence order and shows us when this is true in the narrative.

Rule 2: Time order.
The text and verses are in time order only if says they are as **above**.

Rev 12:1-5

1 And there appeared a great wonder in heaven; a woman clothed with the sun, and the moon under her feet, and upon her head a crown of twelve stars:

2 And she being with child cried, travailing in birth, and pained to be delivered.

3 And there appeared another wonder in heaven; and behold a great red dragon, having seven heads and ten horns, and seven crowns upon his heads.

4 And his tail drew the third part of the stars of heaven, and did cast them to the earth: and the dragon stood before the woman which was ready to be delivered, for to devour her child as soon as it was born.

5 And she brought forth a man child, who was to rule all nations with a rod of iron: and her child was caught up unto God, and to his throne.

Visions are the most difficult to interpret. John is given instructions to write down what he saw which he does to the best of his ability but we know from the idiom "a picture is worth a thousand words" that it is not possible to fully describe all that is seen in a very few words. We therefore are given to understand that the details not told to us are not as important as the vision itself and the connection the vision has with other scripture. We must therefore not interpret the vision with any details not described but with information found elsewhere in scriptures that fits the vision.

Rule 3: Visions must be interpreted using only what is said and prior scripture and not imagination.

Using this rule, we interpret Rev 12:1-5 above as:

1. The woman clothed with the sun, and the moon under her feet, and upon her head a crown of twelve stars is Israel. She is honoured and supported in the heavenlies (by God) and the crown of twelve stars represents the 12 tribes of Israel.
2. She is abought to give birth to a son Jesus Christ.
3. Satan appears in heaven in all his glory
4. Satan entices one third of the angels to follow him and they are cast down on the earth where he joins them, intent on killing Jesus as he is born (using King Herod, Matt 2:13).
5. Jesus Christ who Is to rule all nations with a rod of iron in the millennium was born and then killed but was raised up again by God the father and is now in heaven with Him.

THE END OF THE AGE OF SATAN'S RULE AND THE WRATH OF GOD

From Rev 11:

"17: Saying, We give thee thanks, O Lord God Almighty, which art, and wast, and art to come; because thou hast taken to thee thy great power, and hast reigned.

18 And the nations were angry, and thy wrath is come, and the time of the dead, that they should be judged,

and that thou shouldest give reward unto thy servants the prophets, and to the saints, and them that fear thy name, small and great; and shouldest destroy them which destroy the earth."

From the above two verses we learn that:

1. Verse 17 declares the END OF THE AGE has come and Satan's rule over all the earth is terminated.
2. Verse 18 declares that the time of wrath of God has also come.
3. Verse 18 also declares that it is also time for the dead to be judged and the righteous to be rewarded.
4. Verse 18 also declares that Gods wrath will destroy those who destroyed the earth.

The above all happens when God, in a single moment in time, cancels the covenant he made in Genesis 1:26 with Adam and his progeny to rule over "all the earth" which was then usurped by Satan. From the above we can see that destruction comes to the earth both by man and then from God in judgement and we will have to discern from whom it comes.

We now move on to discern the timing in the "Revelation of Jesus Christ" mentioned above when God terminates Satan's reign and begins his judgements. The judgements described in Rev 11v17 & 18 above that happen at this time are:

1. The dead are to be judged
2. Rewards will be given to his servants the prophets, and the saints, and those that fear his name
3. Gods wrath will destroy those who destroyed the earth

We have found the time we are looking for, it is the time of the resurrection of the dead in Christ or the rapture mentioned in John 5:28-29 which says:

"28 Marvel not at this: for the hour is coming, in the which all that are in the graves shall hear his voice,

29 And shall come forth; they that have done good, unto the resurrection of life; and they that have done evil, unto the resurrection of damnation."

It is also the beginning of God's judgement of those who have done evil to his earth. To establish when this time fits into the revelation of Jesus Christ we are now going to look at who destroys the earth and when.

THE DESTUCTION OF THE EARTH

For reasons of clarity I have moved forward to the judgements of God's wrath mentioned above. These come with the sounding of the seven trumpets in Rev chapter 6 after the opening of the seventh seal. Here we are told the following:

Rev 8:1-7

"1 And when he had opened the seventh seal, there was silence in heaven about the space of half an hour.

2 And I saw the seven angels which stood before God; and to them were given seven trumpets.

3 And another angel came and stood at the altar, having a golden censer; and there was given unto him much incense, that he should offer it with the prayers of all saints upon the golden altar which was before the throne.

4 And the smoke of the incense, which came with the prayers of the saints, ascended up before God out of the angel's hand.

5 And the angel took the censer, and filled it with fire of the altar, and cast it into the earth: and there were voices, and thunderings, and lightnings, and an earthquake.

6 And the seven angels which had the seven trumpets prepared themselves to sound.

7 The first angel sounded, and there followed hail and fire mingled with blood, and they were cast upon the

earth: and the third part of trees was burnt up, and all green grass was burnt up."

Here we see that all the actions are done by angels in heaven and in the presence of God. Here the first tribulation happens after the first angel blows the trumpet and "the third part of trees was burnt up, and all green grass was burnt up". These are clearly God's judgements done by or sanctioned by him.

We now go back in the book of revelations to see Satan and man destroying the earth.

Chapters 2 & 3 contain the letters to the seven churches. Chapter 4v1 starts with "After this I looked, and, behold, a door was opened in heaven: and the first voice which I heard was as it were of a trumpet talking with me; which said, Come up hither, and I will shew thee things which must be hereafter" indicating that a time order is attached to this portion of the vision.

Rev 6:1-4: The opening of the first two seals

1 And I saw when the Lamb opened one of the seals, and I heard, as it were the noise of thunder, one of the four beasts saying, Come and see.

2 And I saw, and behold a white horse: and he that sat on him had a bow; and a crown was given unto him: and he went forth conquering, and to conquer.

3 And when he had opened the second seal, I heard the second beast say, Come and see.

4 And there went out another horse that was red: and power was given to him that sat thereon to take peace from the earth, and that they should kill one another: and there was given unto him a great sword.

Here in contrast to Rev 8:1-7 discussed above there is no evidence of God or his angels doing anything other than showing John what was happening. The rider of the red horse was given power to "take peace from the earth, and that they should kill one another: and there was given unto him a great sword". These actions are completely contrary to the loving God we know as the Prince of Peace. This power was therefore not given by God but by Satan to do evil on and unto the earth precipitating Gods wrath mentioned in chapter 8. For this reason the rider is depicted as riding a red horse (Satan's colour). Here the events described in chapter 6 are not necessary individual events or in time sequence but a collective vision of what Satan, with man's help, is doing to the earth. What we can say is that these events take place prior to the wrath of God being poured out in Rev chapter 8.

Rev 6:12-17: The opening of the sixth seal.

"12 And I beheld when he had opened the sixth seal, and, lo, there was a great earthquake; and the sun became black as sackcloth of hair, and the moon became as blood;

13 And the stars of heaven fell unto the earth, even as a fig tree casteth her untimely figs, when she is shaken of a mighty wind.

14 And the heaven departed as a scroll when it is rolled together; and every mountain and island were moved out of their places.

15 And the kings of the earth, and the great men, and the rich men, and the chief captains, and the mighty men, and every bondman, and every free man, hid themselves in the dens and in the rocks of the mountains;

16 And said to the mountains and rocks, Fall on us, and hide us from the face of him that sitteth on the throne, and from the wrath of the Lamb:

17 For the great day of his wrath is come; and who shall be able to stand?"

Here with opening of the sixth seal the END TIME SIGNS are displayed announcing THE END OF THE AGE and that the wrath of God is at hand. The men who are still alive comprehend the situation and look for ways to escape His wrath.

We now move our gaze to heaven to see what is happening there.

THE EVENTS HAPPENING IN HEAVEN

Rev 6:9-11: Here just before the opening of the sixth seal we see what is happening in heaven.

"9 And when he had opened the fifth seal, I saw under the altar the souls of them that were slain for the word of God, and for the testimony which they held:

10 And they cried with a loud voice, saying, How long, O Lord, holy and true, dost thou not judge and avenge our blood on them that dwell on the earth?

11 And white robes were given unto every one of them; and it was said unto them, that they should rest yet for a little season, until their fellow servants also and their brethren, that should be killed as they were, should be fulfilled."

Here we see the Christian martyrs calling for justice and being told to wait till the final martyr is slain before the wrath of God will avenge them all. From this we understand that Christians who are still to be martyred are still walking on the earth and have not yet been raptured. This indicates a rapture very close to or at the same time as the final judgement. Matt 10:22 "And ye shall be hated of all men for my name's sake: but he that endureth to the end shall be saved" seems to confirm this as we know that Jesus is not referring to the end of the world but the end of the age.

Prior to this in chapter 5 where Jesus is the only one found worthy to open the book with seven seals we are given a glimpse into heaven and see the following:

Rev 5: 6-12

"6 And I beheld, and, lo, in the midst of the throne and of the four beasts, and in the midst of the elders, stood a Lamb as it had been slain, having seven horns and seven eyes, which are the seven Spirits of God sent forth into all the earth.

7 And he came and took the book out of the right hand of him that sat upon the throne.

8 And when he had taken the book, the four beasts and four and twenty elders fell down before the Lamb,

having every one of them harps, and golden vials full of odours, which are the prayers of saints.

9 And they sung a new song, saying, Thou art worthy to take the book, and to open the seals thereof: for thou wast slain, and hast redeemed us to God by thy blood out of every kindred, and tongue, and people, and nation;

10 And hast made us unto our God kings and priests: and we shall reign on the earth.

11 And I beheld, and I heard the voice of many angels round about the throne and the beasts and the elders: and the number of them was ten thousand times ten thousand, and thousands of thousands;

12 Saying with a loud voice, Worthy is the Lamb that was slain to receive power, and riches, and wisdom, and strength, and honour, and glory, and blessing."

Here we see around the throne in verse 8 the "four beasts and four and twenty elders" and angels numbering "ten thousand times ten thousand, and thousands of thousands" but no redeemed souls. Verse 11 again confirms that only the "many angels round about the throne and the beasts and the elders" were there. Here we must not confuse the 24 elders singing and celebrating (with the rest) in verse 10 that he "has made us unto our

God kings and priests: and we shall reign on the earth" as being sung by the redeemed, they are not there. They are singing about a process that is manifesting its self at that moment. So, we can say that although the arrival of the saints is imminent they have not yet arrived by Rev 5 verse 12.

Moving to Rev 7 we are given another glimpse into heaven and see the following:

Rev 7: 8-17

"8 Of the tribe of Zabulon were sealed twelve thousand. Of the tribe of Joseph were sealed twelve thousand. Of the tribe of Benjamin were sealed twelve thousand.

9 After this I beheld, and, lo, a great multitude, which no man could number, of all nations, and kindreds, and people, and tongues, stood before the throne, and before the Lamb, clothed with white robes, and palms in their hands;

10 And cried with a loud voice, saying, Salvation to our God which sitteth upon the throne, and unto the Lamb.

11 And all the angels stood round about the throne, and about the elders and the four beasts, and fell before the throne on their faces, and worshipped God,

12 Saying, Amen: Blessing, and glory, and wisdom, and thanksgiving, and honour, and power, and might, be unto our God for ever and ever. Amen.

13 And one of the elders answered, saying unto me, What are these which are arrayed in white robes? and whence came they?

14 And I said unto him, Sir, thou knowest. And he said to me, These are they which came out of great tribulation, and have washed their robes, and made them white in the blood of the Lamb.

15 Therefore are they before the throne of God, and serve him day and night in his temple: and he that sitteth on the throne shall dwell among them.

16 They shall hunger no more, neither thirst any more; neither shall the sun light on them, nor any heat.

17 For the Lamb which is in the midst of the throne shall feed them, and shall lead them unto living fountains of waters: and God shall wipe away all tears from their eyes."

Here we see in the very next verse after the sealing of the last of the 12 tribes of Israel, a vision of the redeemed already in heaven. The fate of the Israelites who have obviously been left behind will be discussed later. Verse 9 describes a multitude to large to count who are obviously not angels and verse 14 confirms this by telling us that they "came out of great tribulation". Please note that they did not come out of "THE GREAT TRIBULATION" which we have shown does not exist. This multitude includes everyone who has ever suffered tribulation for faithfully serving God including as far back as John the Baptist or even earlier. Immediately after verse 17, where Jesus is attending to the needs of the redeemed who have just arrived in heaven, Jesus opens the seventh seal and we read that there is silence in heaven:

Rev 8: 1-9

"**1** And when he had opened the seventh seal, there was silence in heaven about the space of half an hour.

2 And I saw the seven angels which stood before God; and to them were given seven trumpets.

3 And another angel came and stood at the altar, having a golden censer; and there was given unto him much incense, that he should offer it with the prayers of all saints upon the golden altar which was before the throne.

4 And the smoke of the incense, which came with the prayers of the saints, ascended up before God out of the angel's hand.

5 And the angel took the censer, and filled it with fire of the altar, and cast it into the earth: and there were voices, and thunderings, and lightnings, and an earthquake.

6 And the seven angels which had the seven trumpets prepared themselves to sound.

7 The first angel sounded, and there followed hail and fire mingled with blood, and they were cast upon the earth: and the third part of trees was burnt up, and all green grass was burnt up.

8 And the second angel sounded, and as it were a great mountain burning with fire was cast into the sea: and the third part of the sea became blood;

9 And the third part of the creatures which were in the sea, and had life, died; and the third part of the ships were destroyed."

This silence is because no one in heaven is rejoicing in what is about to happen. In 2 Peter 3:9 the word says "The Lord is not slack concerning his promise, as some men count slackness; but is longsuffering to us-ward, not willing that any should perish, but that all should come to repentance." Here we have come to the most momentous time on God's earth, the time of his wrath and the destruction of the evil men who have destroyed the earth, and Jesus has paused because he did not want to do what he then had to do. We then see the beginning of God's judgements at the sound of the first and second trumpets in verse 7 and 8.

THE EVENTS AND TIMING OF THE GREATEST GLOBAL TRIBULATION EVER

We are now going to view the rapture in the context of the greatest tribulation ever, mentioned already. I have shown above that the rapture occurs before the time of God's final judgement when he pours out his wrath and destruction on the evil men who have destroyed the earth. This is the event I have called "THE GREATEST GLOBAL TRIBULATION EVER" and is triggered by the "abomination of desolation" already mentioned above. Matt 24:15: says "When ye therefore shall see the abomination of desolation, spoken of by Daniel the prophet, stand in the holy place," ….. and Matt 24:21 "For then shall be great tribulation, such as was not since the beginning of the world to this time, no, nor ever shall be." The events leading up to this have already been given in detail and are found in Dan 9:27 & 12:11. Here after a 7 year peace covenant has been agreed, the Antichrist breaks it in the middle of the 7 year period by stopping the daily sacrifice and oblation and then erects an idol called the "abomination of desolation" in the temple's holy of holies in Jerusalem. Here we see the

Antichrist taking God's place in his temple in his city and declaring thereby that he is God and demanding to be worshiped. This is the coup that ends "THIS AGE" and the results are immediate.

Jesus Describes and warns his disciples about this time as follows:

Matt 24:15-22

"15 When ye therefore shall see the abomination of desolation, spoken of by Daniel the prophet, stand in the holy place, (whoso readeth, let him understand:)

16 Then let them which be in Judaea flee into the mountains:

17 Let him which is on the housetop not come down to take anything out of his house:

18 Neither let him which is in the field return back to take his clothes.

19 And woe unto them that are with child, and to them that give suck in those days!

20 But pray ye that your flight be not in the winter, neither on the sabbath day:

21 For then shall be great tribulation, such as was not since the beginning of the world to this time, no, nor ever shall be.

22 And except those days should be shortened, there should no flesh be saved: but for the elect's sake those days shall be shortened."

Here Jesus, speaking to his disciples, makes it clear that when they see or know of the idol in the temple that blasphemes God and makes desolate, they must leave the Judean area immediately and flee into the mountains, if they wish to survive. There are no mountains near Jerusalem just inhabited hills. The nearest safe area would be caves around Engedi or Qumran in the Judean wilderness. This is about 50km away and a 10 hour walk away at 5km per hour, the maximum one can do with children, pregnant wives and extended family.

The person "on the housetop" is told that he does not have time to enter his house. He will need to walk 10 km to get a reasonable distance out of town, not even to a safe place and this will take a minimum of 2 hours with children and family. The person "in the field" is told is told that he does not have time to return to his house.

If he is 2 km on the far side of the old city, he will only be about 7 Km from the city after 2 hours.

If we use the half hour period of silence in heaven (Rev 8:1) as a guide and assume that this is the time God waits before acting, then everyone in Judaea has half an hour to escape to the hills.

While this not possible for those in Jerusalem they can at least get 2.5 km away from the city if they leave immediately. The judgement of God starts with the opening of the seventh seal (Rev 8: 1) and an earthquake (Rev 8: 5). Considering that you want to be at least 2km from the epicentre and away from buildings to survive even a moderate earthquake they do not have time linger.

CAN WE PREDICT THE SEASON AND TIME OF THE RAPTURE?

Jesus does not want any of his beloved servants to be left behind and so warns us to be alert for the rapture in Luke 21v34 "And take heed to yourselves, lest at any time your hearts be overcharged with surfeiting, and drunkenness, and cares of this life, and so that day come upon you unawares." This indicates that we can know when the rapture is imminent and in verse 36 we are also told how we may escape this time if we are found worthy. In Luke 21V36 Here Jesus says "Watch ye therefore, and pray always, that ye may be accounted worthy to escape all these things that shall come to pass, and to stand before the Son of man." Here we must not see this as an instruction to lock ourselves in a room and fast and pray but rather to being alert to the signs and circumstances of the day and listening for Holy Spirit prophecies and praying for the Holy Spirit to direct your escape as He did for the church in AD70. If we love the Lord even till death, know the scriptures and are waiting, longing for his appearing, we will find ourselves in the right place at the right time.

To answer the question above we can say that as soon as the Antichrist makes the 7 year peace agreement with the Jews, we will know the Rapture will take place 3.5 years later and we should be able to name the month in which it will take place. We may also be able name the day of the rapture if the cancellation of the 7 year peace agreement and the ceremony for setting up the "abomination of desolation" idol is announced in advance. But we will have no other warning because Rev 3v3 says "If therefore thou shalt not watch, I will come on thee as a thief, and thou shalt not know what hour I will come upon thee" confirming that the rapture precedes the heavenly signs announcing the END OF THE AGE.

POST RAPTURE PERIOD

As detailed above the rapture occurs in a moment of time before the wrath of God is poured out at the 'END

OF THE AGE' which is triggered and announced by the "abomination of desolation" idol appearing in the 3rd Jewish temple. Rev 7 verse 9 tells us that those raptured will come from all the nations and therefore includes the born-again Jews.

Rev 7v9. "After this I beheld, and, lo, a great multitude, which no man could number, of all nations, and kindreds, and people, and tongues, stood before the throne, and before the Lamb, clothed with white robes, and palms in their hands"

Everyone who's name is written in the Lamb's book of life will be raptured to be with the Lord. Those that remain, the nations and including the unredeemed Jews, will go through the greatest period of tribulation ever. This book is intended to alert Christians to Satan's ploy to lead them into the false assurance of the rapture preceding the end time tribulation and thereby trapping and destroying them through their unpreparedness. The events concerning the remaining Jews is a study on its own and if given here will detract and dilute the main message. It suffices to say that the Lord has a special plan for his brothers the Jews and 144000 of them are marked and given special protection and there is also a way of physical escape made available for them.

Rev 7:4 "And I heard the number of them which were sealed: and there were sealed an hundred and forty and four thousand of all the tribes of the children of Israel."

Rev 12:6 "And the woman fled into the wilderness, where she hath a place prepared of God, that they should feed her there a thousand two hundred and threescore days." (1260days = 42 months = 3.5 years = The second half of the 7 year peace covenant)

It is not clear from scripture if there will be any salvation or rapture events after the end of the age rapture, except for the 2 witnesses mentioned in Rev 11v3. "And I will give power unto my two witnesses, and they shall prophesy a thousand two hundred and threescore days, clothed in sackcloth" (The 1260 days is the same 3.5 years, the second half of the 7 year peace covenant) mentioned in the paragraph above. These 2 witnesses will preach for the full period after the end of the age rapture then themselves be raptured. Rev 11v12 "And they heard a great voice from heaven saying unto them, Come up hither. And they ascended up to heaven in a cloud; and their enemies beheld them."

3
CHAPTER

A TIME ORDERED SUMMARY OF MY FINDINGS

1. The period of great Christian tribulation has existed from the time John the Baptist had his head removed and will increase in frequency as we get closer to the end of the age, due both with the population increase, and the increase in lawlessness. There will be no end to Christian tribulation till the 'END OF THE AGE' rapture occurs.

2. The Antichrist will agree a 7 year peace treaty with Israel which will allow the Israelis to build the 3rd temple or at least Moses' Tent of Meeting.

3. In the middle of this 7 year period the Antichrist will cancel the agreement and place the abomination of desolation idol in the Jewish temple. (Matt 24:15: "stand in the holy place").

4. This is the sign of the 'END OF THE AGE' and causes an immediate reaction from God. This is where Jesus says to his disciples in Matt 24:17 that they will not even have time to fetch their clothes in the house before God's wrath is poured out on Jerusalem and Judea.

5. It is the time of the final judgement when the wrath of God is poured out on the earth and is also the time of the rapture. The rapture is therefore very close to or at the same time as the final judgement. We know however, that the rapture will precede the END TIME SIGNS of the judgement to come on all the earth because we know that when Jesus appears in the sky to collect his elect he comes like a thief in the night. (Luke 12:40)

6. The GREATEST GLOBAL TRIBULATION EVER begins with the appearance of the abomination of desolation idol in the holy place of the Jewish temple.

7. The end of the GREATEST GLOBAL TRIBULATION EVER comes after about 3.5 years, but the precise end time is not clear. We know that God has shortened this period

because otherwise no one would have survived (Matt 24:22) and we are told in Dan 12:11 that a time of 1290 days (43 months) will be counted after the start of The GREATEST GLOBAL TRIBULATION EVER begins. While this looks to be the end, verse 12 seems to contradict this saying that those who "wait" (survive) till the 1335th day (a further 45 days) will count themselves blessed.

8. After the end of the GREATEST TRIBULATION EVER the signs of the Lord's second coming are displayed and then he appears in the sky and the millennium, the 1000 years of peace on earth begins. Matt 24v 29: says "Immediately after the tribulation of those days shall the sun be darkened, and the moon shall not give her light, and the stars shall fall from heaven, and the powers of the heavens shall be shaken: 30: And then shall appear the sign of the Son of man in heaven: and then shall all the tribes of the earth mourn, and they shall see the Son of man coming in the clouds of heaven with power and great glory."

4

CHAPTER

CONCLUSIONS

The main conclusion of this study is that there is NO so called 7 year period of great tribulation that all Christians will escape because the rapture will precede it.

Note that this book has been written from the Christian point of view and therefore does not illuminate the End Times Events affecting only the Jews. Its main purpose is to reveal the deception currently circulating from eminent bible preachers that all Christians will escape the 7 YEAR GREAT TRIBULATION by being raptured before it happens. I have found that there is no 7 YEAR GREAT TRIBULATION but only a constantly increasing persecution of Christian believers from the beheading of John the Baptist to the worst of all persecutions which occurs during our last 3 and a half years on earth. This happens when the Antichrist makes a seven year peace covenant with the Jews in Jerusalem and then concentrates his hate and anger on all believing Christians. They are raptured without warning 3.5 years later at the time the Antichrist erects the abomination of desolation idol in the new Jewish temple/tent. This causes God to terminate man and Satan's rule over all the earth, bringing about the END OF THIS AGE. His wrath is then poured out on all the earth.

All Christians therefore need to know that there will be no easy ride and that their faith will be tested till the last day. They will just have to trust the Lord and hang in there till the rapture occurs.

The End Times Time Table can be categorised as follows:

John the Baptist to seven year peace covenant: constantly increasing persecution of Christians (2000 years)

Seven year peace covenant till rapture: Worst persecution of Christians ever (3.5 years)

Rapture: Jesus collects all his true believers in the sky

Silence in heaven for half an hour

The SIGNS appear in the heavens of Gods imminent judgement of those who destroyed the earth.

Gods judgements are poured out on the earth (3.5 years)

ADENDUM: WHO IS GOING TO HEAVEN AND HOW TO MAKE SURE THAT YOU ESCAPE THE GREATEST TRIBULATION EVER AND JOIN JESUS IN HEAVEN

Not everyone is going to heaven. Revelation 21 verses 6 to 8 says the following:

"**6** And he said unto me, It is done. I am Alpha and Omega, the beginning and the end. I will give unto him that is athirst of the fountain of the water of life freely.

7 He that overcometh shall inherit all things; and I will be his God, and he shall be my son.

8 But the fearful, and unbelieving, and the abominable, and murderers, and whoremongers, and sorcerers, and idolaters, and all liars, shall have their part in the lake which burneth with fire and brimstone: which is the second death."

We see from verse 7 that we have to do something to inherit the kingdom of Heaven, we have to overcome. And what do we have to overcome? We have to overcome any or all the things mentioned in verse 8 which means that if we have just once given in to fear or unbelief, never mind the rest, we are already disqualified. This makes it impossible for anyone to get in by their own effort but not for God. You see that already in verse 7, the verse that says you have to overcome, it is already pointing to Gods solution by telling that you inherit the kingdom of Heaven. In other words you can't earn it, you get it because of your relationship with your father. We can now explain that the things in verse 8 that keep you out of heaven are Satanic and not acceptable in heaven. Jesus is simply telling you that you have to be a lover of God and hater of Satan to be acceptable in heaven. Here we must not lose heart because God has a magnificent plan for our salvation and it is called JESUS and he wrote these words to us in John 3 verses 16 & 17:

"For God so loved the world, that he gave his only begotten Son, that whosoever believeth in him should not perish, but have everlasting life. For God sent not his Son into the world to condemn the world; but that the world through him might be saved."

So we can confirm that God wants you in Heaven, so how do you get there? Fortunately, he also shows us the way.

THE WAY OF SALVATION

Firstly, you need to decide that you want to be with Jesus in Heaven.

Secondly, you need to decide that you do not want to serve Satan any more but be righteous even as Jesus is righteous in Heaven.

You can achieve this because the scriptures declare in John 1 verses 8 to 9:

"**8** If we say that we have no sin, we deceive ourselves, and the truth is not in us.

9 If we confess our sins, he is faithful and just to forgive us our sins, and to cleanse us from all unrighteousness."

Also the word says in Romans 10 verses

"**8** But what saith it? The word is nigh thee, even in thy mouth, and in thy heart: that is, the word of faith, which we preach;

9 That if thou shalt confess with thy mouth the Lord Jesus, and shalt believe in thine heart that God hath raised him from the dead, thou shalt be saved.

10 For with the heart man believeth unto righteousness; and with the mouth confession is made unto salvation."

So if you confess to Jesus that you have sinned and you also confess that he is Lord of your life you will be saved. Now all you have to do is pray the prayer below aloud and mean it and salvation is yours.

SINNERS PRAYER (say aloud)

DEAR LORD JESUS I ACKNOWLEDGE THAT I HAVE SINNED AND ASK YOU TO FORGIVE ALL MY SINS, PAST, PRESENT AND FUTURE. I ASK YOU TO BE MY LORD AND SAVOUR AND LIVE WITH ME FOREVER MORE.

If you have said this prayer I welcome you into the body of Christ. All the angels in heaven are rejoicing over your salvation. You are however still a baby in Christ and will need good food to grow strong. Please read the next section "How to become a strong Christian".

HOW TO BECOME A STRONG CHRISTIAN

Do the following. The order of importance is from top to bottom.

1. Get a bible. I only quote from the King James Version (also called authorised version, best if you can understand it), or New King James (2nd best) or American Standard Version.
2. Read and study it every day.
3. Find a church that believes Jesus is God and believes in baptism in water and also baptism in the Holy Spirit.
4. Join a bible study group.

5. Get baptised in water.
6. Get baptised in the Holy Spirit.
7. Get a concordance. A Crudence paper back will do.
8. Get a commentary. A Hodder Bible Handbook or similar will do but read your bible and study it before using the hand book.

Printed in the United States
By Bookmasters